SECURE YOUR FUTURE

A PRACTICAL GUIDE TO FINANCIAL LITERACY

By

Nick Imoru

Achievers Publishing
Calgary, Canada

SECURE YOUR FUTURE: A PRACTICAL GUIDE TO FINANCIAL LITERACY
Copyright © 2024 By Nicholas Imoru

ISBN: 978-1-989291-10-8

Published in Canada, by
Achievers Publishing

Canadian Cataloguing in Publication (CIP)
A Record of this Publication is available from the Library and Archives Canada (LAC).

For further information or permission, address:
Achievers Publishing
Calgary, Canada
E-mail: info@achieverspublishing.com
www.achieverspublishing.com

Printed in Canada for Achievers Publishing

SECURE YOUR FUTURE

A PRACTICAL GUIDE TO FINANCIAL LITERACY

Dedication

This book is lovingly dedicated to my pastor, Pastor Emmanuel Akinola, and his beautiful wife, Deaconess Julie Akinola, of Winners Chapel International, Americas.

Your unwavering dedication to the Word of God, your exemplary leadership, and your heartfelt commitment to empowering lives have been a constant source of inspiration. Your teachings and guidance have laid the foundation for many to secure not only their spiritual future but also their earthly success.

Thank you for being shining examples of faith, wisdom, and stewardship. May God continue to bless and enlarge your ministry as you impact countless lives for His glory.

Table of Contents

Contents

Introduction

In recent years, financial instability has become a common reality for many individuals and families across North America. Despite living in two of the wealthiest countries in the world—Canada and the United States—many struggle with managing their personal finances effectively. The statistics tell a sobering story that highlights this growing problem.

According to surveys and research, the financial issues faced by Canadians and Americans have become increasingly difficult to manage, affecting their overall well-being.

These statistics reveal a disturbing trend: financial stress is becoming a daily burden for many individuals, both in Canada and the U.S. The widespread lack of savings and investments, coupled with overwhelming debt, leaves millions unprepared for financial emergencies, let alone their retirement years.

The Bible reflects on the wisdom of preparation and saving. Proverbs 21:20 (NIV) declares: *"The wise store up choice food and olive oil, but fools gulp theirs down."* This scripture teaches us that prudent planning and saving are essential practices, especially in a world where financial uncertainty is a growing reality.

The Importance of Financial Literacy

The core of many financial problems in North America stems from a lack of financial education. Schools often neglect to teach essential money management skills. As a result, many individuals enter adulthood unprepared to handle credit cards, loans, and other financial products. Without this foundational knowledge, people may easily fall into debt or misuse their savings.

In **Canada** and **the U.S.**, debt has become an ingrained way of life. For many, it starts right after college with large student loans. Credit cards, car loans, and mortgages often follow, weighing heavily on families. Living paycheck to paycheck has sadly become the norm for millions. As Proverbs 22:7 (NIV) warns: *"The* *rich rule over the poor, and the borrower is slave to the lender.*" This scripture highlights the danger of falling into a debt cycle, where individuals become beholden to their creditors.

Financial literacy is the key to breaking free from these burdens. It equips individuals with the knowledge and skills needed to budget, save, invest, and make informed decisions about their money. When individuals understand the basics of how money works, they can plan more effectively and avoid the traps that lead to financial distress.

In today's world, it's easy to be overwhelmed by the abundance of financial products and the vast amounts of advice available. From credit cards and loans to insurance and investment accounts, the financial landscape can be confusing. But at the core of this complexity is a simple truth: financial literacy is not about mastering every product but about understanding the basics. The ability to **budget**, **save**, **invest**, and **protect your money** is essential to financial success.

Purpose of the Book

This book is designed to simplify the often overwhelming world of personal finance. It offers a practical and easy-to-understand guide for managing your money effectively. Rather than delving into complex financial jargon, this book focuses on the fundamentals—how money works—so that you can make better financial decisions.

We aim to:

- Grab your attention and ignite your interest in financial matters.

- Help you understand the basics of saving, investing, and wealth-building.

- Encourage you to take control of your financial future.

The Bible reminds us that no one is more invested in our financial well-being than ourselves. As Proverbs 13:11 (NIV) teaches: "*Dishonest money dwindles away, but whoever gathers money little by little makes it grow.*" This principle reinforces the need for steady, disciplined savings and planning to secure a brighter financial future.

As you embark on this journey of financial education, always remember - no one cares more about your financial future than you do. Not the government, not your employer. It's your responsibility to learn the basic rules of how money works, to take care of your family, and to build a solid financial foundation. The power lies in your hands, and with the right knowledge, you can shape a secure and prosperous future.

PART 1: UNDERSTANDING YOUR FINANCIAL HEALTH

Chapter 1: The State of Financial Affairs

Financial Statistics in Canada and the U.S.

The financial landscape in North America presents a picture that is both sobering and eye-opening. Many individuals and families struggle to maintain financial security, despite the considerable wealth and resources available in Canada and the United States. The statistics from both countries provide a stark reminder of how important financial literacy and preparedness are for long-term well-being.

In Canada, the financial situation of many citizens reveals a concerning trend:

- 35% of Canadians do not have any savings or investments.

- Only 27% of private-sector workers have access to employer-funded pension plans, leaving the majority of Canadians responsible for saving and investing for their retirement.

- The average savings in Registered Retirement Savings Plans (RRSPs) is a mere $55,000—a sum that is far from adequate to support a comfortable retirement.

Meanwhile, in the United States, the financial statistics reveal a similar, if not more alarming, reality:

- 33% of Americans, representing over 77 million people, do not pay their bills on time.

- 39% of Americans carry credit card debt from month to month, struggling to pay off balances that often come with high-interest rates.

- Only 59% of U.S. adults report having any savings at all, and many lack an emergency fund to fall back on.

- Even more troubling is that more than half of Americans now believe it's acceptable to default on their mortgage if they cannot afford to pay it.

These statistics paint a troubling picture of financial instability across North America. Despite living in two of the wealthiest countries in the world, millions of people are financially unprepared, struggling to make ends meet, and ill-equipped to handle emergencies or plan for retirement.

Proverbs 21:20 (NIV) advises: *"The wise store up choice food and olive oil, but fools gulp theirs down."* This verse speaks to the wisdom of preparation and prudent financial management, encouraging individuals to plan for the future by setting aside resources.

Common Financial Struggle

The financial challenges faced by Canadians and Americans are often rooted in three primary areas: debt, lack of savings, and poor financial planning.

1. Debt: A Growing Burden

Debt has become a way of life for many in North America, beginning as early as college and persisting throughout adulthood. In Canada, student loans, credit cards, mortgages, and car loans are just a few examples of the financial obligations that weigh heavily on families. In the United States, the burden of debt is equally prevalent, with many individuals struggling to pay down large balances while incurring additional debt each month.

The consequences of carrying significant debt are severe. Interest payments can eat away at income, preventing individuals from saving for future goals. Proverbs 22:7 (NIV) says, *"The rich rule over the poor, and the borrower is slave to the lender."* This verse highlights the reality of debt bondage, where individuals find themselves trapped in a cycle of repayment, unable to build wealth or achieve financial freedom.

Debt is particularly challenging when paired with insufficient income or poor financial habits, which leads to a pattern of borrowing just to make ends meet. Many individuals fall into the habit of living beyond their means, relying on credit to fund a lifestyle they cannot afford. As debt piles up, it becomes increasingly difficult to break free from this cycle, leading to long-term financial hardship.

2. Lack of Savings: Unprepared for Emergencies

In both Canada and the United States, the lack of adequate savings is a pervasive issue. Without a financial cushion, individuals are vulnerable to unexpected expenses, such as medical bills, car repairs, or job loss. The statistics show that a significant portion of the population does not have enough savings to cover even minor financial emergencies.

In Canada, where 35% of the population lacks any savings or investments, many individuals are living paycheck to paycheck, unable to plan for the future. Similarly, in the United States, 39% of Americans carry credit card debt month to month, often using their credit cards to cover daily expenses because they do not have sufficient savings.

The Bible teaches the importance of storing up resources for the future. Proverbs 6:6-8 (NIV) offers wisdom on preparation: *"Go to the ant, you sluggard; consider its ways and be wise! It has no commander, no overseer or ruler, yet it stores its provisions in summer and gathers its food at harvest."* This scripture illustrates the importance of setting aside savings during times of abundance so that you are prepared for times of need.

3. Poor Financial Planning: Failing to Prepare for the Future

Another key factor contributing to financial struggles is poor planning. Many individuals do not take the time to create a budget or develop a long-term financial strategy, which leaves them vulnerable to financial setbacks. In both Canada and the United States, there is a widespread lack of understanding regarding personal finance management.

Without a budget, it is difficult to track spending, save consistently, or prioritize financial goals. Individuals who do not budget often find themselves spending more than they earn, leading to debt accumulation and financial stress. In the absence of proper planning, even high earners can struggle financially, as they fail to manage their money wisely.

Planning for the future is essential, particularly when it comes to retirement. In both Canada and the United States, many workers are unprepared for retirement, relying too heavily on government programs like

Social Security or the Canada Pension Plan. However, these programs alone are not enough to provide financial security in retirement, and without additional savings, many individuals face financial difficulties later in life.

Luke 14:28 (NIV) says: "*Suppose one of you wants to build a tower. Won't you first sit down and estimate the cost to see if you have enough money to complete it?*" This verse emphasizes the importance of planning ahead—whether for building a tower or securing your financial future. Without careful consideration and foresight, financial plans may crumble under the weight of unexpected challenges.

In summary, understanding the financial statistics and common struggles in North America—such as debt, lack of savings, and poor financial planning—helps us recognize the urgent need for better financial literacy. The next step is to learn how to take control of your financial health, plan for the future, and break free from the cycles that keep you financially insecure.

Chapter 2: Assessing Your Financial Situation

Understanding Income vs. Expenses

The first step toward gaining control of your finances is understanding the relationship between your income and expenses. Many people live paycheck to paycheck, not fully grasping where their money goes each month. To take control of your financial situation, it's essential to develop a clear understanding of your cash flow—how much money is coming in versus how much is going out.

Income refers to all the money you receive regularly, whether from a job, business, investments, or other sources. Your income is the foundation upon which you build your financial future, as it determines how much you can save, invest, and spend.

Expenses, on the other hand, are all the ways in which you spend your money. Expenses can be divided into two categories:

1. **Fixed expenses**: These are consistent costs that recur every month, such as rent or mortgage payments, utilities, and insurance.

2. **Variable expenses**: These fluctuate depending on your lifestyle and spending habits, including groceries, transportation, entertainment, and dining out.

The key to managing your finances successfully is ensuring that your **income exceeds your expenses**. While this might sound simple, many people fail to track their spending carefully, leading to financial imbalances. **Impulse buying** and **lifestyle inflation** (increasing spending as income rises) are common traps that can derail even the best-intentioned financial plans.

To avoid financial pitfalls, it's crucial to create and maintain a **budget**. A budget allows you to allocate your income toward essential expenses, savings, and financial goals, while also keeping discretionary spending in check. Proverbs 21:5 (NIV) warns: *"The plans of the diligent lead to profit as surely as haste leads to poverty."* This scripture reminds us of the importance of careful financial planning and the risks of uncontrolled spending.

A practical way to start assessing your income and expenses is by listing all your sources of income and categorizing your expenses. Many financial experts recommend the **50/30/20 rule**, which allocates 50% of income to necessities, 30% to wants, and 20% to savings and debt repayment. This simple framework can help you balance your financial obligations while still enjoying some flexibility in your spending.

Once you understand where your money is going, you can make informed decisions about cutting back on unnecessary expenses and reallocating funds toward your savings and future goals. **Self-discipline** is essential here, as it helps you stick to your budget and prevent overspending.

Calculating Your Net Worth

Once you've gained clarity on your income and expenses, the next step in assessing your financial situation is calculating your **net worth**. Your net worth is one of the most critical indicators of your financial health, as it represents the difference between what you **own** (assets) and what you **owe** (liabilities).

What is Net Worth?

Simply put, **net worth** is the sum of all your assets minus your liabilities:

- **Assets** are everything you own that has value, such as your cash, savings, investments (stocks, bonds, RRSPs, 401(k)s), real estate (your home), and valuable possessions (cars, jewelry, etc.).

- **Liabilities** are the debts and obligations you owe, such as credit card balances, mortgages, student loans, car loans, and other personal debts.

Net Worth Equation: Net Worth = Assets – Liabilities

For example, if you own a home worth $200,000 but owe $150,000 on your mortgage, your net worth for that asset is $50,000. Similarly, if you have $10,000 in savings and investments but owe $5,000 in credit card debt, your net worth from these sources is $5,000.

When you subtract all your liabilities from your assets, you arrive at your **total net worth**. Your net worth can be either **positive** (if your assets exceed your liabilities) or **negative** (if your liabilities exceed your assets). A positive net worth means you are accumulating wealth, while a negative net worth indicates financial challenges that need to be addressed.

Why is Net Worth Important?

Your **net worth** is a vital measure of your overall financial stability. It provides a snapshot of where you stand financially at any given moment and helps you track your progress over time. The goal should be to steadily increase your net worth by paying down debt, saving more, and growing your assets through investments and smart financial decisions.

Proverbs 27:23 (NIV) offers wise counsel: *"Be sure you know the condition of your flocks, give careful attention to your herds."* In modern terms, this verse encourages us to stay on top of our financial situation and manage our assets wisely.

Tracking your net worth on a regular basis can help you stay motivated and focused on achieving your long-term financial goals. By knowing your current financial standing, you can make more informed decisions about budgeting, investing, and debt repayment. Many people use tools like spreadsheets or financial apps like Mint or Personal Capital to monitor their net worth and keep their finances organized.

Steps to Calculate Your Net Worth:

1. **List your assets**: Gather information on all your savings accounts, investments, real estate, and other valuables. Be sure to include any accounts that generate passive income, such as rental properties or dividends.

2. **List your liabilities**: Write down all the debts and financial obligations you owe, including your mortgage, credit card balances, student loans, car loans, and any other outstanding liabilities.

3. **Subtract liabilities from assets**: Once you have an accurate list of both, subtract the total amount of your liabilities from the total amount of your assets. The result is your current net worth.

Improving Your Net Worth

If your net worth is lower than you'd like, don't be discouraged. There are several steps you can take to improve it over time:

- **Reduce debt**: Start by paying down high-interest debt, such as credit cards. As your liabilities decrease, your net worth will improve.

- **Increase savings**: Commit to saving a portion of your income each month. Even small contributions can grow significantly over time, thanks to compound interest.

- **Invest wisely**: Investing in assets like stocks, bonds, or real estate can help grow your wealth faster than keeping your money in a traditional savings account.

It's important to remember that building wealth and increasing your net worth is a gradual process that requires discipline and patience. As Proverbs 13:11 (NIV) advises: *"Dishonest money dwindles away, but whoever gathers money little by little makes it grow."* This verse reminds us that wealth accumulation is not about quick fixes or get-rich-quick schemes. Instead, it's about making consistent, wise choices that yield long-term financial security.

In conclusion, assessing your financial situation by understanding your income, expenses, and net worth is a foundational step toward achieving financial stability. By gaining clarity on your cash flow and financial health, you can begin making informed decisions that will help you grow your wealth, reduce debt, and build a more secure future.

Chapter 3: The Reality of Debt

Debt is a reality that affects millions of individuals and families across North America. While it can be a useful tool for making large purchases, such as buying a home or financing an education, debt also carries significant risks. Understanding the various types of debt and how to manage and reduce it is essential for maintaining financial health. In this chapter, we will explore different types of debt, strategies for reducing debt, and common financial pitfalls to avoid.

Types of Debt

Debt comes in many forms, and each type has its own terms, benefits, and risks. Understanding the nature of each type of debt can help you make better decisions about borrowing and repayment.

1. Credit Card Debt

Credit card debt is one of the most common forms of debt and also one of the most dangerous. Credit cards offer convenience and flexibility, allowing you to make purchases and pay them off over time. However, they often come with high-interest rates, which can make it easy to fall into a cycle of debt.

Many individuals use credit cards for everyday expenses, often spending beyond their means. The average credit card interest rate can range from 15% to over 25%, making it difficult to pay off balances if you only make minimum payments.

Proverbs 22:7 (NIV) warns us: *"The rich rule over the poor, and the borrower is slave to the lender."* This verse reflects the reality of credit card debt, where high-interest payments can trap individuals in a cycle of borrowing and repayment.

2. Student Loans

For many young adults, student loans are the first significant financial obligation they face. While education is an important investment in the future, the cost of attending college or university has risen dramatically in both Canada and the United States. This has led to a substantial increase in student loan debt.

Student loans generally offer lower interest rates than credit cards, but the debt can still be overwhelming. In Canada, student loans are often tied to government programs, while in the U.S., both federal and private loans are common. Repayment typically begins after graduation, but for many graduates, finding a job that pays enough to cover both living expenses and student loan payments is a challenge.

Proverbs 3:13-14 (NIV) tells us: *"Blessed are those who find wisdom, those who gain understanding, for she is more profitable than silver and yields better returns than gold."*

This scripture encourages individuals to seek education and knowledge but also highlights the need to balance the financial cost of obtaining that wisdom.

3. Car Loans

Car loans are another common form of debt. Vehicles are essential for many people, particularly in areas with limited public transportation options. However, car loans can be expensive, especially if you finance a new or luxury vehicle.

Car loans typically have terms ranging from three to seven years, with interest rates varying based on your credit score and the lender. While having a car may be a necessity, it's important to choose a vehicle that fits within your budget. Borrowing more than you can afford can lead to financial strain, as monthly payments for car loans can take up a significant portion of your income.

4. Mortgages

A **mortgage** is a type of debt used to finance the purchase of a home. Unlike credit card debt or car loans, mortgages are considered "good debt" because they are used to acquire an asset—your home—that can appreciate in value over time. Mortgages typically have lower interest rates than other types of debt and can span decades (usually 15 to 30 years).

While a mortgage can help you achieve homeownership, it is still important to be cautious when taking on this type of debt. Buying a home that is beyond your means or taking out a large mortgage can leave you financially vulnerable if unexpected circumstances arise.

How to Manage and Reduce Debt

Managing and reducing debt requires discipline and strategic planning. Without a clear plan, debt can quickly spiral out of control, leading to financial stress and long-term consequences. Here are some key strategies for managing and reducing debt effectively.

1. Create a Budget and Prioritize Debt Repayment

A well-structured budget is essential for managing your finances, especially when you have debt. Start by listing all your income sources and expenses, then allocate a portion of your income toward paying off your debt each month. This helps ensure you are consistently reducing your debt, rather than letting it grow.

Debt prioritization is a technique that involves focusing on the most expensive or high-interest debt first. For instance, paying down credit card balances (which typically have high-interest rates) should be a priority over lower-interest debts like student loans or mortgages.

2. Use the Debt Snowball or Debt Avalanche Method

Two popular strategies for paying off debt are the debt snowball and debt avalanche methods.

- The **debt snowball method** involves paying off the smallest debts first while making minimum payments on larger debts. Once a small debt is paid off, you move on to the next smallest, and so on. This method can provide psychological motivation as you see your debts disappear one by one.

- The **debt avalanche method** focuses on paying off the debts with the highest interest rates first. This approach can save you more money in the long run, as it reduces the amount of interest you'll pay over time.

Romans 13:8 (NIV) reminds us: "*Let no debt remain outstanding, except the continuing debt to love one another, for whoever loves others has fulfilled the law.*" This scripture encourages us to eliminate financial debt as soon as possible, so we can live free of burdens and focus on what truly matters.

3. Avoid New Debt

One of the most critical steps in reducing debt is avoiding new debt. Resist the temptation to take on additional loans or use credit cards for unnecessary purchases. This may require lifestyle adjustments, such as cutting back on discretionary spending or finding additional income sources.

4. Consolidate Debt (If Applicable)

Debt consolidation is an option for individuals with multiple high-interest debts. By combining several debts into a single loan with a lower interest rate, you can make repayment more manageable. Consolidation can help simplify your financial obligations and potentially reduce the total amount of interest you pay.

Avoiding Common Financial Pitfalls

Many people fall into financial traps that worsen their debt situation. Being aware of these pitfalls can help you avoid unnecessary financial struggles and stay on track toward financial freedom.

1. Impulse Buying

Impulse buying is one of the biggest contributors to excessive debt. It's easy to make unplanned purchases with credit cards, especially when retailers offer attractive deals and discounts. However, these small purchases can quickly add up, leading to a growing credit card balance. Learning to resist impulse buying is critical to staying within your budget.

Proverbs 21:17 (NIV) warns: *"Whoever loves pleasure will become poor; whoever loves wine and olive oil will never be rich."* This scripture reminds us that indulging in excess and unnecessary purchases can prevent us from achieving true financial prosperity.

2. Using Debt for Non-Essential Expenses

Taking on debt for non-essential expenses, such as vacations or luxury items, can be a major financial mistake. While it may seem harmless to put these expenses on a credit card or take out a loan, it can lead to long-term financial hardship if you are unable to pay off the debt quickly.

3. Not Having an Emergency Fund

Without an emergency fund, unexpected expenses can lead to more debt. Medical bills, car repairs, or job loss can put a strain on your finances if you don't have savings to cover these events. Building an emergency fund with at least three to six months' worth of living expenses can protect you from needing to rely on credit cards or loans when unexpected costs arise.

In conclusion, debt is a reality that most people will face at some point in their lives. By understanding the different types of debt and how to manage them effectively, you can avoid the pitfalls of excessive borrowing and build a more secure financial future. With discipline, a clear repayment strategy, and a focus on reducing your liabilities, you can take control of your financial health and work toward debt freedom.

PART 2: BUDGETING AND MANAGING YOUR MONEY

Chapter 4: Creating and Sticking to a Budget

Budgeting is the cornerstone of financial health. A well-planned budget allows you to track your income, manage your expenses, and allocate money toward savings and financial goals. However, the real challenge often lies in not only creating a budget but sticking to it. In this chapter, we will explore the key steps to creating an effective budget, understanding the difference between needs and wants, and practical tips for sticking to a budget, especially when dealing with the constraints of a student budget.

Differentiating Between Needs and Wants

One of the most important aspects of budgeting is learning to distinguish between **needs** and **wants**. Misunderstanding this difference can often lead to overspending and financial stress.

Needs

Needs are essential expenses that you cannot avoid. These include:

- **Housing** (rent or mortgage payments)
- **Utilities** (electricity, water, gas)
- **Groceries** (basic food supplies)
- **Transportation** (car payments, public transit)
- **Healthcare** (insurance, medications)

These expenses are necessary for survival and maintaining a basic quality of life. When creating a budget, needs should always be your top priority.

Wants

Wants, on the other hand, are expenses that you can live without but may enhance your lifestyle. These include:

- **Dining out** or ordering takeout
- **Entertainment** (movies, concerts, streaming services)
- **Luxury items** (designer clothing, gadgets)

- **Vacations** or leisure travel

While it's okay to spend money on wants, they should be managed carefully, especially if you are working with a limited income or trying to save for specific goals. Being able to differentiate between needs and wants is crucial for budgeting success.

Proverbs 21:17 (NIV) offers a biblical perspective on managing desires: *"Whoever loves pleasure will become poor; whoever loves wine and olive oil will never be rich."* This verse reminds us that constant indulgence in unnecessary desires can lead to financial instability.

Once you clearly define your needs and wants, you can make informed decisions about where to allocate your money, ensuring that your essential needs are met before spending on discretionary items.

Steps to Create a Budget

Creating a budget might seem daunting at first, but it is a simple and effective tool for managing your finances. A budget helps you keep track of where your money is going, ensures that you cover your basic needs, and allows you to plan for future goals. Here are the essential steps to creating a practical budget:

1. Track Your Income

The first step in creating a budget is to determine your total monthly income. This includes your salary, wages from part-time work, or any other income sources, such as rental income or freelance work. If your income varies from month to month, use an average based on the last several months to get an accurate estimate.

If you are a student, your income may come from different sources, such as part-time jobs, student loans, or financial support from family members. Be sure to include all sources of income when planning your budget.

2. List Your Expenses

Next, make a list of all your monthly expenses. Start with your fixed expenses—those that remain the same every month, such as rent, loan payments, or insurance premiums. Then, list your variable expenses, such as groceries, transportation, utilities, and discretionary spending (dining out, entertainment, etc.).

Categorize these expenses as **needs** or **wants**. This will help you prioritize your spending and identify areas where you might be able to cut back if necessary.

3. Set Financial Goals

After identifying your income and expenses, it's important to set financial goals. These can include short-term goals, such as saving for a vacation or paying off a credit card, and long-term goals, like building an emergency fund or saving for retirement.

By setting goals, you create a purpose for your budget, which makes it easier to stay motivated. Your goals should be **SMART**—specific, measurable, achievable, relevant, and time-bound.

4. Allocate Your Income

Once you've listed your expenses and set your goals, it's time to allocate your income to cover your needs, wants, and savings. Many financial experts recommend the **50/30/20 rule** as a starting point:

- **50%** of your income should go toward **needs** (housing, food, transportation).

- **30%** can be allocated to **wants** (entertainment, dining out).

- **20%** should go to **savings** and **debt repayment**.

Adjust these percentages based on your personal financial situation. For instance, if you have high student loan debt, you may need to allocate more than 20% of your income to debt repayment until you get your balance under control.

5. Adjust as Needed

Life is unpredictable, and your financial situation may change over time. It's important to review your budget regularly and make adjustments as necessary. If your income increases, allocate more toward savings or paying down debt. If unexpected expenses arise, temporarily cut back on discretionary spending to stay on track.

Tips for Sticking to a Budget

Sticking to a budget can be challenging, especially for students who may have limited income and significant financial obligations. However, with discipline and a few smart strategies, it's possible to stay within your budget and even save money while managing your education expenses. Here are some practical tips:

1. Automate Your Savings

One of the best ways to ensure that you stick to your budget is by automating your savings. Set up automatic transfers from your checking account to a savings account as soon as you receive your income. This way, you're "paying yourself first" and ensuring that you're setting aside money for future goals without having to think about it.

Proverbs 13:11 (NIV) reminds us: *"Dishonest money dwindles away, but whoever gathers money little by little makes it grow."* Even small savings can grow over time through consistency and discipline.

2. Cut Back on Non-Essential Spending

As a student, it can be tempting to spend on non-essential items like takeout, coffee, or entertainment. However, cutting back on these expenses can free up more money for savings or important purchases. Try preparing meals at home, taking advantage of student discounts, or opting for free entertainment options.

3. Use Budgeting Tools and Apps

There are many budgeting apps available that can help you keep track of your spending and stick to your budget. Apps like Mint or YNAB (You Need a Budget) allow you to set spending limits in different categories, track expenses in real-time, and get notifications when you're approaching your budget limits.

4. Plan for Unexpected Expenses

Unexpected expenses, such as car repairs or medical bills, can throw off your budget if you're not prepared. Set aside a small portion of your income each month for an **emergency fund**. Even if you can only save a little, having some money set aside for emergencies will help you avoid using credit cards or taking on additional debt.

5. Prioritize Debt Repayment

If you have student loans or credit card debt, prioritize paying down these balances as quickly as possible. Consider using the debt snowball or debt avalanche method to tackle your debt systematically. By reducing your debt burden, you'll free up more of your income for savings and discretionary spending.

6. Find Ways to Increase Income

If your budget is tight, consider finding ways to increase your income. Look for part-time jobs, freelance opportunities, or side hustles that can supplement your earnings. Even small additional sources of income can help ease financial pressure and give you more flexibility in your budget.

In conclusion, creating and sticking to a budget is essential for managing your finances effectively. By understanding the difference between needs and wants, following the steps to create a budget, and employing practical strategies to stay on track, you can take control of your money and work toward achieving your financial goals. With discipline, persistence, and a clear plan, budgeting can help you build a stable financial future.

Chapter 5: Turning Spending into Saving

For many people, the key to achieving financial security lies in the ability to control spending and turn that money into savings. This process requires self-discipline, careful tracking of expenditures, and a clear understanding of how to reduce unnecessary costs. In this chapter, we will explore practical techniques for controlling spending and strategies for reducing non-essential expenses. By implementing these techniques, you can gradually transform your spending habits and start building the savings you need for financial success.

Techniques for Controlling Spending

Controlling spending is often the most challenging part of managing personal finances. Without self-discipline and a clear strategy for tracking expenses, it's easy to lose sight of where your money is going. Fortunately, there are several techniques that can help you take control of your spending habits and put your finances back on track.

1. Self-Discipline: The Foundation of Financial Control

At the heart of controlling spending is self-discipline. Self-discipline allows you to say no to unnecessary purchases and make responsible financial decisions, even when faced with temptation. It is a skill that can be developed with practice, and it plays a crucial role in achieving financial freedom.

Self-discipline is about doing what is necessary even when it isn't easy. Whether it's choosing to save money instead of buying something on impulse or delaying gratification to meet long-term goals, self-discipline is essential for maintaining a healthy financial life. As you develop this skill, you will find it easier to stay within your budget, build savings, and avoid debt.

Proverbs 25:28 (NIV) provides a biblical perspective on self-control: *"Like a city whose walls are broken through is a person who lacks self-control."* Without self-discipline, financial walls—your budget, savings, and financial goals—can easily crumble, leaving you vulnerable to unnecessary spending.

2. Track Your Expenditures

One of the most effective ways to control spending is by tracking where your money goes. By keeping a detailed record of your expenditures, you gain visibility into your spending patterns, allowing you to identify areas where you might be overspending.

To get started, write down every expense, no matter how small, for a week or a month. Categorize your spending into essential and non-essential items. This will help you see how much money you are spending on things like dining out, entertainment, and other discretionary purchases.

Budgeting tools and apps can make tracking expenses easier. Apps like Mint, YNAB (You Need a Budget), or even a simple spreadsheet can help you log your expenses, categorize them, and see trends in your spending habits. When you can see where your money is going, it becomes easier to make adjustments and control unnecessary expenses.

3. Set Spending Limits

Another practical way to control spending is by setting **spending limits** for certain categories of your budget. For example, you might allocate a specific amount of money for entertainment, dining out, or shopping each month. Once you reach the limit, you stop spending in that category until the next month.

Setting spending limits creates a built-in system of accountability, helping you stay within your budget. It also forces you to prioritize your spending and think carefully before making purchases. Over time, these small adjustments can lead to significant savings.

Ways to Reduce Unnecessary Expenses

Reducing unnecessary expenses is an important step in turning spending into savings. By cutting back on non-essential costs, you free up more of your income to put toward savings, investments, or debt repayment. Here are several strategies to help you reduce unnecessary spending without sacrificing your quality of life.

1. Cut Back on Dining Out and Takeout

One of the easiest ways to reduce unnecessary expenses is to cut back on dining out and takeout. While it can be convenient to grab a meal from a restaurant or order food delivery, these costs add up quickly. Preparing meals at home is significantly more cost-effective and can also be healthier.

If you find it difficult to cook at home regularly, start by reducing the number of times you eat out each week. For example, you could aim to dine out only once or twice a week and prepare simple meals at home the rest of the time. Over the course of a month, this small change can lead to significant savings.

2. Cancel Unused Subscriptions

With the rise of streaming services, gym memberships, and subscription boxes, it's easy to accumulate multiple subscriptions that you rarely use. These recurring expenses can quickly drain your finances if you're not paying attention.

Take some time to review your subscriptions and cancel any that you don't use regularly. For example, if you have multiple streaming services, consider keeping only one. If you rarely go to the gym, look for free or lower-cost alternatives, such as exercising at home or outdoors.

Proverbs 21:20 (NIV) says: "*The wise store up choice food and olive oil, but fools gulp theirs down.*" This verse reflects the importance of being prudent and avoiding waste, especially when it comes to managing your resources wisely.

3. Shop with a List

Impulse buying can be a major contributor to overspending. One way to combat this is by creating a shopping list before you go to the store. Whether you're grocery shopping or buying household items, having a list helps you stay focused on what you actually need, rather than being tempted by sales or items you don't plan to buy.

By sticking to your list, you can reduce impulse purchases and save money on items that aren't essential. Over time, this simple habit can have a big impact on your spending and help you build better financial habits.

4. Look for Discounts and Coupons

Another way to save money is by looking for discounts, coupons, and sales before making purchases. Many stores offer promotions or loyalty programs that can help you save on essential items like groceries, clothing, and household goods. By taking advantage of these deals, you can reduce the overall cost of your purchases.

Additionally, online shopping platforms often offer price comparison tools, allowing you to find the best deal on an item before making a purchase. By making a habit of seeking out discounts and comparing prices, you can significantly reduce unnecessary spending over time.

5. Reduce Energy Costs

Another area where you can cut back on expenses is your energy bills. Simple changes, such as turning off lights when not in use, using energy-efficient appliances, and adjusting your thermostat, can lead to lower utility bills. Consider unplugging electronics when they are not in use, as some devices continue to use power even when turned off.

By making your home more energy-efficient, you can reduce your utility costs while also benefiting the environment.

In conclusion, turning spending into saving requires self-discipline, careful tracking of expenditures, and a commitment to reducing unnecessary expenses. By implementing practical techniques such as setting spending limits, cooking at home, and cutting out non-essential costs, you can free up more money to put toward savings and long-term financial goals. As Proverbs 13:11 (NIV) reminds us, "*Whoever gathers money little by little makes it grow.*" Small changes in your spending habits can lead to significant financial growth over time, helping you build a more secure financial future.

Chapter 6: Emergency Funds and Planning for the Unexpected

Life is unpredictable, and financial emergencies can strike at any time. Whether it's an unexpected medical bill, a car repair, or a sudden job loss, having a financial safety net is crucial to avoiding debt and staying financially secure. An emergency fund is your first line of defense against these unplanned expenses. In this chapter, we will explore why having an emergency fund is essential, and how to build and maintain one to prepare for life's financial surprises.

Why an Emergency Fund is Crucial

An emergency fund serves as a financial cushion to protect you when unexpected expenses arise. It ensures that you have readily accessible money to cover emergencies without having to rely on credit cards, loans, or other forms of debt. The importance of an emergency fund cannot be overstated, as it provides peace of mind and financial stability in times of crisis.

1. Financial Security During Emergencies

One of the main reasons an emergency fund is crucial is that it offers financial security. Emergencies can happen when we least expect them—whether it's a health issue, a car breakdown, or even a sudden loss of income. Without an emergency fund, many people turn to credit cards or loans, which can quickly accumulate interest and lead to long-term debt.

By having an emergency fund, you are equipped to handle these unexpected expenses without jeopardizing your financial health. Proverbs 27:12 (NIV) wisely reminds us: *"The prudent see danger and take refuge, but the simple keep going and pay the penalty."* This verse emphasizes the importance of foresight and preparation, especially in the context of financial management.

2. Avoiding Debt and High-Interest Payments

Without an emergency fund, people are often forced to borrow money or use high-interest credit cards to cover emergency expenses. This can lead to a cycle of debt that becomes difficult to escape. For example, if you rely on a credit card with a 20% interest rate to cover a $2,000 emergency, the resulting debt can grow rapidly if not paid off quickly.

An emergency fund helps you avoid this situation by providing liquid cash that can be accessed without taking on additional debt. This keeps your financial situation stable and prevents interest payments from eroding your wealth over time.

3. Flexibility and Peace of Mind

An emergency fund also provides peace of mind. Knowing that you have money set aside for emergencies allows you to focus on your long-term financial goals without worrying about potential setbacks. Whether you're saving for retirement, investing, or building wealth, having an emergency fund gives you the flexibility to stay on course, even when life throws unexpected challenges your way.

Moreover, it offers emotional relief. Many people experience stress and anxiety when faced with sudden financial challenges. With an emergency fund in place, you can handle these situations calmly and with confidence, knowing that your finances are secure.

How to Save for Unexpected Financial Situations

Building an emergency fund takes time and discipline, but the benefits far outweigh the effort. Here are practical steps to help you start saving for unexpected financial situations and maintain a robust emergency fund.

1. Set a Savings Target

The first step in building an emergency fund is to set a **savings target**. Most financial experts recommend saving enough to cover **three to six months' worth of living expenses**. This includes essential costs such as rent or mortgage payments, utilities, groceries, and transportation.

If three to six months' expenses seem daunting, start with a smaller goal, such as saving $1,000 as an initial cushion. Once you reach that milestone, continue to build your emergency fund gradually until you achieve your larger goal.

Proverbs 21:5 (NIV) offers wisdom on saving diligently: *"The plans of the diligent lead to profit as surely as haste leads to poverty."* This scripture encourages us to be patient and persistent in our efforts, knowing that consistent, small contributions can lead to significant financial stability over time.

2. Automate Your Savings

One of the best ways to ensure you consistently save for your emergency fund is to **automate your savings**. Set up automatic transfers from your checking account to a dedicated savings account each time you receive your paycheck. This way, saving becomes effortless, and you won't be tempted to spend the money before it's set aside for emergencies.

Consider setting up your automatic transfers for a specific percentage of your income, such as 10%, or a fixed amount each month. Even small contributions will add up over time, and automating the process helps you stay committed to your savings goals.

3. Keep Your Emergency Fund Separate

It's important to keep your emergency fund in a **separate savings account** from your regular spending accounts. This ensures that the money is reserved exclusively for emergencies and not used for everyday expenses or discretionary purchases.

Consider opening a **high-yield savings account** for your emergency fund. This type of account allows your money to grow with interest while still being easily accessible in case of emergencies. Avoid keeping your emergency fund in investments like stocks, which can fluctuate in value and may not be readily available when needed.

4. Cut Back on Non-Essential Spending

To build your emergency fund quickly, consider cutting back on **non-essential spending**. Look for areas in your budget where you can reduce expenses, such as dining out, entertainment, or luxury purchases. Redirect the money you save from these categories into your emergency fund.

Even small adjustments in your spending habits can make a big difference over time. For example, brewing your coffee at home instead of buying it at a café can save you hundreds of dollars a year, all of which can go directly into your savings.

5. Use Windfalls Wisely

If you receive an unexpected windfall, such as a tax refund, work bonus, or gift, consider using it to boost your emergency fund. Windfalls provide a great opportunity to make significant progress toward your savings goal without affecting your regular budget.

While it might be tempting to spend a windfall on non-essential items, prioritizing your emergency fund can provide long-term financial benefits and protect you from future financial stress.

6. Replenish Your Fund After Use

If you need to dip into your emergency fund, it's important to replenish it as soon as possible. Once the emergency is over and your finances stabilize, make a plan to rebuild your fund by resuming regular contributions. Having a fully-funded emergency account ensures that you're prepared for the next unexpected event.

Biblical Principles of Preparation and Stewardship

The Bible offers timeless wisdom on the importance of preparation and financial stewardship. Proverbs 6:6-8 (NIV) illustrates this concept beautifully: "*Go to the ant, you sluggard; consider its ways and be wise! It has no commander, no overseer or ruler, yet it stores its provisions in summer and gathers its food at harvest.*" This passage teaches us the value of foresight and diligent preparation. Just as the ant stores food for the future, we are encouraged to save and prepare for life's uncertainties.

By saving for emergencies, we practice good stewardship over the resources God has entrusted to us. It ensures that we are not caught unprepared in times of crisis and that we can maintain financial stability without relying on debt or external assistance.

In conclusion, an emergency fund is a crucial element of financial planning. It provides a safety net that allows you to face life's unexpected challenges without falling into debt or financial instability. By setting savings goals, automating contributions, and cutting back on non-essential spending, you can build an emergency fund that offers both security and peace of mind. With discipline and diligence, you can protect yourself from financial setbacks and stay on track toward achieving your long-term financial goals.

PART 3: GROWING YOUR WEALTH

Chapter 7: Building Wealth through Smart Investments

Investing is one of the most powerful tools available to grow wealth and achieve long-term financial security. While saving money in a bank account can protect you from financial emergencies, investing your money allows it to grow and compound over time, providing a path to financial independence. In this chapter, we will explore the basics of stocks, bonds, and mutual funds, highlight the importance of long-term investing, and delve into key strategies like dollar-cost averaging and asset allocation.

Overview of Stocks, Bonds, and Mutual Funds

Understanding the different types of investments available is essential to building wealth. Each investment vehicle—stocks, bonds, and mutual funds—offers unique advantages, risks, and potential returns. Knowing how they work will help you make informed decisions and diversify your investment portfolio.

1. Stocks

Stocks represent ownership in a corporation. When you buy a share of a company's stock, you essentially become a part-owner of that company. This entitles you to a portion of the company's assets and earnings. Stocks can be a powerful investment tool because they have the potential to provide high returns over time, especially if the company performs well.

Stocks are typically divided into two categories:

- **Common stocks**: These give shareholders voting rights at company meetings and a share of the company's profits through dividends.

- **Preferred stocks**: These usually offer higher fixed dividend payments and priority over common shareholders in the event of liquidation, but they do not carry voting rights.

While stocks have the potential for high returns, they also come with higher risks. Stock prices can be volatile, influenced by market conditions, company performance, and economic factors.

Luke 19:13 (NIV) provides biblical insight into the concept of stewardship and investing: "*So he called ten of his servants and gave them ten minas. 'Put this money to work,' he said, 'until I come back.'*" This passage encourages us to invest wisely, using the resources we've been given to multiply and grow over time.

2. Bonds

Bonds are essentially loans made by investors to corporations or governments. When you purchase a bond, you are lending money to the issuer in exchange for regular interest payments, and the principal amount is returned at the bond's maturity.

Bonds are generally considered safer investments than stocks because they provide fixed, predictable income. However, they typically offer lower returns compared to stocks. Bonds are an excellent option for those seeking a more stable investment, particularly for those nearing retirement or with lower risk tolerance.

3. Mutual Funds

A **mutual fund** is a pool of money collected from many investors to invest in a diversified portfolio of stocks, bonds, or other securities. Mutual funds are managed by professional fund managers who decide how to allocate the fund's assets to achieve the fund's objectives.

Mutual funds offer several advantages:

- **Diversification**: By investing in a variety of assets, mutual funds reduce the risk of losses from any single investment.

- **Accessibility**: Investors can buy shares in a mutual fund with a relatively small initial investment, making it accessible to those who want to diversify their portfolios but lack the capital to invest in individual stocks or bonds.

There are various types of mutual funds, including:

- **Stock funds**: These invest primarily in stocks and offer the potential for higher returns, but with more risk.

- **Bond funds**: These invest in bonds and provide a more stable income, with less risk.

- **Balanced funds**: These invest in a combination of stocks and bonds, providing a balance between growth and income.

Proverbs 13:11 (NIV) teaches: *"Dishonest money dwindles away, but whoever gathers money little by little makes it grow."* Investing in mutual funds reflects this principle of gradual, steady wealth-building over time.

The Importance of Long-Term Investing

Long-term investing is the key to growing wealth. While it can be tempting to chase quick profits by frequently buying and selling investments, the most successful investors are those who take a **long-term approach**. This strategy allows your investments to grow and benefit from **compound interest** over time.

1. The Power of Compounding

Compounding is the process by which the earnings from an investment are reinvested to generate additional earnings. Over time, this creates a snowball effect, as your money begins to grow exponentially. The longer your investments remain untouched, the more powerful compounding becomes.

For example, if you invest $10,000 at a 7% annual return, your investment will grow to approximately $19,672 in ten years, even if you don't contribute any additional funds. After 20 years, the same $10,000 would grow to $38,697. This demonstrates the importance of **time** when it comes to investing— starting early and staying patient allows your money to work for you.

2. Reducing the Impact of Market Volatility

The stock market can be volatile in the short term, with prices fluctuating due to economic changes, political events, or company performance. However, over the long term, the market tends to grow, making it a more reliable investment. By staying invested for the long term, you can ride out the ups and downs of the market and benefit from overall growth.

Ecclesiastes 11:2 (NIV) advises: *"Invest in seven ventures, yes, in eight; you do not know what disaster may come upon the land.*" This biblical principle reflects the importance of diversification and long-term planning, encouraging investors to spread risk across various investments.

Dollar-Cost Averaging and Asset Allocation

Two key strategies for managing investment risk while maximizing returns are dollar-cost averaging and asset allocation. These approaches help investors navigate market volatility and build a balanced portfolio.

1. Dollar-Cost Averaging

Dollar-cost averaging involves investing a fixed amount of money at regular intervals, regardless of the asset's price. By investing consistently, you purchase more shares when prices are low and fewer shares when prices are high, lowering your average cost per share over time.

This strategy takes the emotion out of investing and reduces the risk of trying to time the market. It's especially effective for long-term investors who want to accumulate wealth gradually without worrying about market fluctuations.

For example, if you invest $100 in a stock each month, sometimes you'll buy when prices are high, and other times when prices are low. Over time, this approach averages out the cost of your investments, allowing you to take advantage of lower prices during market downturns.

Ecclesiastes 11:6 (NIV) reflects this principle of steady, disciplined investment: "*Sow your seed in the morning, and at evening let your hands not be idle, for you do not know which will succeed, whether this or that, or whether both will do equally well.*" By investing consistently, regardless of market conditions, you increase your chances of success over time.

2. Asset Allocation

Asset allocation refers to the process of dividing your investments among different asset classes, such as stocks, bonds, and cash, to balance risk and reward. The ideal asset allocation depends on your financial goals, risk tolerance, and time horizon.

- **Stocks** provide growth potential but come with higher risk.

- **Bonds** offer stability and income, with lower risk but lower returns.

- **Cash** provides liquidity but does not grow over time.

By diversifying across different asset classes, you reduce the risk that a downturn in one area will significantly impact your overall portfolio. As you approach major financial goals (such as retirement), you may want to shift your allocation to more conservative investments like bonds to preserve your wealth.

It's important to regularly review and adjust your asset allocation to ensure it aligns with your changing financial goals and market conditions.

In conclusion, building wealth through smart investments requires a solid understanding of stocks, bonds, and mutual funds, as well as the discipline to invest for the long term. Strategies like dollar-cost averaging and asset allocation help manage risk while maximizing returns. By staying invested, diversifying your portfolio, and letting your money compound over time, you can grow your wealth steadily and achieve your financial goals. Proverbs 21:20 (NIV) says, "*The wise store up choice food and olive oil, but fools gulp theirs down.*" This wisdom reminds us that careful planning and consistent investing lead to lasting prosperity.

Chapter 8: Understanding Compound Interest

One of the most powerful concepts in personal finance is **compound interest**. Whether you are saving, investing, or paying off debt, compound interest can significantly impact your financial future. By understanding how it works, you can harness its potential to grow your wealth over time. In this chapter, we will explore the power of compound interest, how it works in your favor, and provide practical examples of growing your savings through the power of interest.

The Power of Compound Interest and How It Works in Your Favor

Compound interest is often referred to as the "eighth wonder of the world" because of its ability to multiply wealth over time. Unlike simple interest, which is calculated only on the initial amount (the principal), compound interest is calculated on both the initial principal and the accumulated interest from previous periods. This means that your money earns interest on interest, creating a snowball effect that grows your savings exponentially over time.

How Compound Interest Works

The formula for calculating compound interest is:

$$A = P(1+r/n)^{nt}$$

Where:

- **A** = the future value of the investment/loan, including interest

- **P** = the principal investment amount (initial deposit or loan amount)

- **r** = the annual interest rate (decimal)

- **n** = the number of times that interest is compounded per year

- **t** = the time the money is invested or borrowed for, in years

In this formula, the more frequently interest is compounded, the more your money will grow over time. For example, interest that is compounded annually will grow slower than interest compounded monthly or daily.

The key to maximizing the benefits of compound interest is **time**. The longer your money is invested or saved, the more opportunities it has to grow through compounding. This is why starting early is one of the best financial decisions you can make.

Proverbs 13:11 (NIV) reflects this principle: *"Dishonest money dwindles away, but whoever gathers money little by little makes it grow."* This verse highlights the importance of consistent, patient effort in growing wealth, which is exactly what compound interest provides.

How Compound Interest Works in Your Favor

The beauty of compound interest is that it can work in your favor when saving or investing. Here's how:

- **Savings Accounts**: When you deposit money into a savings account that earns compound interest, the bank pays you interest not only on your initial deposit but also on the interest it has already paid. Over time, this can lead to substantial growth in your savings, even with modest contributions.

- **Investment Growth**: If you invest in stocks, bonds, or mutual funds, compound interest applies not only to the returns on your initial investment but also to the reinvested returns. This allows your investment to grow exponentially over the long term.

For example, let's say you invest $1,000 in an account that earns 5% interest compounded annually. After one year, your account would grow to $1,050. The following year, you would earn 5% not just on the original $1,000, but on the new total of $1,050, resulting in $1,102.50. As the years go by, this compounding effect continues to accelerate, significantly boosting your overall wealth.

Practical Examples of Growing Savings with Interest

To understand the real power of compound interest, let's look at some practical examples of how savings can grow over time using compound interest. These examples will demonstrate how even small, consistent contributions can lead to substantial financial growth when combined with compound interest.

Example 1: Starting Early with Modest Contributions

Imagine you start saving $100 per month in a high-yield savings account with an annual interest rate of 6%, compounded monthly. Here's how your savings would grow over time:

- After 10 years: Your total contributions would amount to $12,000, but with compound interest, your savings would grow to approximately $16,470.

- After 20 years: Your total contributions would be $24,000, but your savings would grow to $47,227.

- After 30 years: Your total contributions would be $36,000, but thanks to compound interest, your savings would grow to $100,451.

As you can see, the longer you let your money compound, the more dramatic the growth becomes. Even modest contributions can lead to significant savings when compounded over a long period.

Ecclesiastes 11:2 (NIV) offers wise advice on long-term financial planning: "*Invest in seven ventures, yes, in eight; you do not know what disaster may come upon the land.*" This verse encourages us to invest wisely and diversify over time, trusting in gradual growth and the benefits of compounding.

Example 2: The Cost of Delaying Savings

Now, let's look at what happens if you delay saving. Suppose you wait 10 years before starting to save, contributing the same $100 per month at 6% interest. After 20 years of saving, your total savings would amount to about $47,227—the same amount that someone who started 10 years earlier had after just 20 years.

This example illustrates the cost of procrastination. By waiting, you miss out on the compounding growth that could have occurred in those 10 lost years. This demonstrates why it is essential to start saving and investing as early as possible.

Example 3: The Power of Higher Interest Rates

The power of compound interest becomes even more impressive with higher interest rates. Consider an investment of $10,000 in an account with a 10% annual interest rate, compounded annually:

- After 10 years: The initial $10,000 would grow to approximately $25,937.

- After 20 years: The investment would grow to about $67,275.

- After 30 years: The investment would grow to a remarkable $174,494.

As this example shows, higher interest rates can significantly boost your wealth when combined with compounding. However, it's important to remember that higher returns often come with higher risks, especially when investing in stocks or mutual funds.

Harnessing Compound Interest for Financial Freedom

The power of compound interest is one of the greatest financial tools available, and it can be harnessed by anyone, regardless of income level. By starting early, making consistent contributions, and allowing time to work in your favor, you can achieve financial freedom and long-term security.

To make the most of compound interest, consider the following steps:

- **Start saving or investing as early as possible**, even if the amount is small.

- **Choose accounts or investments that offer compound interest**, such as high-yield savings accounts, bonds, or mutual funds.

- **Reinvest your earnings** rather than withdrawing them, allowing your investments to continue growing.

- **Be patient**—the longer you let your money grow, the more powerful compounding becomes.

In conclusion, compound interest is a powerful force that can help you grow your wealth exponentially over time. By understanding how it works and implementing practical saving and investing strategies, you can make your money work for you and achieve financial success. As Proverbs 21:5 (NIV) wisely teaches, *"The plans of the diligent lead to profit as surely as haste leads to poverty."* With diligence, patience, and the power of compound interest, you can build a secure financial future that continues to grow throughout your lifetime.

Chapter 9: Generating Multiple Streams of Income

Relying on a single source of income can leave you vulnerable to financial instability, especially in the event of job loss, economic downturns, or unexpected life changes. To safeguard your financial future and build wealth, it's essential to diversify your income sources. In this chapter, we will explore why generating multiple streams of income is important and discuss various income-generating strategies, such as side hustles, freelancing, and other opportunities that can help you achieve financial independence.

Why It's Important to Diversify Income Sources

Diversifying your income is a key principle of financial security and wealth building. It involves creating multiple ways to earn money, so that if one income source is disrupted, you still have others to rely on. This strategy not only provides financial stability, but it also allows you to increase your overall earnings, enabling you to save, invest, and reach your financial goals more quickly.

1. Reducing Financial Risk

One of the main benefits of diversifying your income sources is that it helps reduce financial risk. If all your income comes from a single source, such as a full-time job, you are completely dependent on that job for your financial well-being. Losing that job due to downsizing, economic changes, or unforeseen circumstances can leave you in a vulnerable position.

By creating multiple streams of income, you minimize the impact of losing one source. If your primary income source is disrupted, you can rely on your other streams to maintain financial stability until you find a replacement.

Ecclesiastes 11:2 (NIV) offers timeless wisdom on this matter: *"Invest in seven ventures, yes, in eight; you do not know what disaster may come upon the land."* This verse highlights the importance of diversifying your financial ventures to protect against unforeseen circumstances.

2. Accelerating Wealth Building

Multiple streams of income allow you to accelerate your wealth-building efforts. When you have more than one source of income, you can increase your savings, pay off debt faster, and invest more money, which will ultimately help you achieve your financial goals more quickly.

For example, in addition to your full-time job, you might start a side business, invest in real estate, or take on freelance work. Each additional stream of income contributes to your overall financial picture, providing more resources to allocate toward long-term wealth-building strategies.

3. Gaining Financial Independence

Diversifying your income streams is also a pathway to financial independence. Financial independence occurs when you have enough income from various sources—such as investments, businesses, and passive income streams—that you no longer rely on a traditional job to cover your living expenses.

When you achieve financial independence, you gain the freedom to spend your time on activities that are meaningful to you, whether that's pursuing your passions, traveling, or spending more time with family. Generating multiple income streams is a critical step toward achieving this level of financial freedom.

Side Hustles, Freelancing, and Other Income-Generating Strategies

There are countless ways to create additional streams of income, and the best strategy depends on your skills, interests, and available time. Below are some popular and effective methods for generating extra income outside of your primary job.

1. Side Hustles

A side hustle is any type of work or business that you pursue in addition to your full-time job. Side hustles can be a great way to earn extra income, especially if you have a specific skill or hobby that you can monetize. The beauty of side hustles is that they are often flexible and can be done on your own time, allowing you to balance them with your regular job.

Examples of side hustles include:

- **Tutoring or teaching**: If you have expertise in a particular subject, you can offer tutoring services to students or even teach online courses.

- **Delivery services**: Working as a delivery driver for companies like 'Uber Eats' or 'DoorDash' allows you to earn money on your own schedule.

- **Renting out assets**: If you own a property, vehicle, or equipment, you can rent it out to others. Platforms like Airbnb make it easy to rent out a spare room or entire home.

- **Selling products**: You can start a small online business selling products you create or source, such as handmade crafts, artwork, or clothing.

Proverbs 12:11 (NIV) provides insight into the value of hard work: *"Those who work their land will have abundant food, but those who chase fantasies have no sense."* This verse reminds us that consistent effort in building income-generating activities can lead to fruitful rewards.

2. Freelancing

Freelancing is another excellent way to create an additional stream of income. As a freelancer, you offer your services to clients on a project-by-project basis, often working independently. Freelancers have the flexibility to choose their clients, set their rates, and control their work schedules.

Freelancing opportunities are abundant in various fields, including:

- **Writing and editing**: If you have strong writing skills, you can offer freelance writing, editing, or content creation services to businesses, websites, or individuals.

- **Graphic design**: If you are skilled in design, you can take on freelance projects to create logos, marketing materials, or websites for clients.

- **Consulting**: Professionals with expertise in areas such as finance, marketing, or technology can offer consulting services to businesses that need guidance.

- **Programming and web development**: Freelance programmers and web developers are in high demand to build websites, apps, and software for clients.

Freelancing allows you to leverage your existing skills to earn additional income, often at higher rates than traditional employment. It also gives you the opportunity to build a client base and establish a reputation that could lead to even more opportunities.

3. Passive Income Streams

Passive income is income that you earn without actively working for it on a day-to-day basis. While passive income streams often require an initial investment of time or money, they continue to generate income with minimal ongoing effort. Some popular passive income streams include:

- **Investing in stocks or dividends**: Purchasing dividend-paying stocks can provide you with regular income from the dividends, even as your investments appreciate in value.

- **Real estate investing**: Investing in rental properties can generate monthly rental income, while the property itself may increase in value over time.

- **Creating digital products**: If you have knowledge in a particular area, you can create digital products, such as eBooks, courses, or software, that can be sold repeatedly online.

- **Affiliate marketing**: By promoting products or services through affiliate programs, you can earn commissions when people make purchases through your referral links.

Passive income streams are particularly valuable because they continue to generate earnings without requiring your constant involvement. Over time, building multiple passive income streams can lead to financial independence and long-term wealth.

4. Investing in Real Estate

Real estate investing is a popular and proven strategy for creating wealth. By purchasing properties and renting them out to tenants, you can generate passive rental income. Additionally, properties tend to appreciate over time, providing long-term financial gains through equity growth.

There are several ways to get started with real estate investing:

- **Rental properties**: Purchasing residential or commercial properties to rent out can generate a steady stream of income.

- **House flipping**: Buying undervalued properties, renovating them, and then selling them at a higher price can yield significant profits if done correctly.

- **Real estate crowdfunding**: For those who don't want the responsibility of managing a property, real estate crowdfunding platforms allow you to invest in real estate projects alongside other investors.

Real estate investing requires an upfront investment and careful planning, but it can be an effective way to build wealth and diversify your income sources.

In conclusion, generating multiple streams of income is a key strategy for reducing financial risk, accelerating wealth building, and gaining financial independence.

By exploring side hustles, freelancing, passive income streams, and real estate investments, you can diversify your income and build a more secure financial future. As Proverbs 24:27 (NIV) advises, *"Put your outdoor work in order and get your fields ready; after that, build your house."* This scripture reminds us to lay a strong foundation through diligent work and preparation, ensuring that our financial future is built on multiple, stable sources of income.

PART 4: SECURING YOUR FINANCIAL FUTURE

Chapter 10: The Importance of Financial Independence

Achieving financial independence is a significant goal for many individuals who seek the freedom to live life on their own terms without being constrained by financial worries. While financial freedom and financial independence are often used interchangeably, they are distinct concepts with different levels of control over one's financial destiny. In this chapter, we will explore the difference between financial freedom and financial independence and outline the steps necessary to achieve lasting financial independence.

The Difference Between Financial Freedom and Independence

Understanding the difference between financial freedom and financial independence is key to setting clear financial goals and developing a long-term strategy for success.

1. Financial Freedom

Financial freedom refers to having enough financial resources to cover all your essential needs and wants, while still maintaining a level of financial security. A person who achieves financial freedom has the ability to spend money on things that improve their quality of life without worrying about how to cover basic expenses. Financial freedom typically involves:

- Being free from high-interest debt (such as credit card debt).

- Having enough savings to handle financial emergencies.

- Being able to comfortably cover your living expenses, such as housing, utilities, food, and transportation.

In essence, financial freedom means you are not living paycheck to paycheck, and you can afford to make choices that align with your values and goals without experiencing financial stress. However, financial freedom doesn't necessarily mean you are free from working or generating income.

Proverbs 22:7 (NIV) captures the essence of financial freedom: *"The rich rule over the poor, and the borrower is slave to the lender."* This scripture reminds us that true freedom begins when we are no longer bound by debt, which is often a barrier to financial freedom.

2. Financial Independence

Financial independence, on the other hand, takes financial freedom a step further. It means having enough wealth and passive income to cover all your living expenses without the need to work. Someone who is financially independent is no longer reliant on active income (such as a salary) to meet their financial obligations.

Financial independence allows you to make life choices that are not dictated by the need to earn money. Whether you want to retire early, travel the world, start a passion project, or spend more time with family, financial independence gives you the freedom to live your life according to your own schedule and desires.

The goal of financial independence is to have multiple streams of income, such as investments, rental properties, or passive business earnings, that consistently cover your living expenses, allowing you to live off your investments instead of your labor. While financial freedom provides security, financial independence provides complete freedom of choice.

Steps to Achieve Financial Independence

Achieving financial independence requires a well-thought-out plan and the discipline to stay on track with long-term financial goals. Here are key steps to help you achieve financial independence:

1. Define Your Financial Goals

The first step toward achieving financial independence is to clearly define what financial independence looks like for you. Ask yourself questions such as:

- How much money will I need to cover my living expenses without working?

- What does my ideal financially independent lifestyle look like?

- At what age do I want to achieve financial independence?

By defining your financial goals, you set a clear target that will guide your savings, investments, and financial decisions going forward.

Be sure to calculate your financial independence number—the total amount of wealth you need to generate enough passive income to cover your annual expenses. A common rule of thumb is the **4% rule**, which suggests that you can safely withdraw 4% of your investment portfolio each year in retirement. To calculate your financial independence number, multiply your annual expenses by 25. For example, if your annual expenses are $40,000, you would need $1,000,000 invested to achieve financial independence.

2. Build a Strong Financial Foundation

Before you can focus on achieving financial independence, it's essential to build a strong financial foundation. This includes:

- **Paying off high-interest debt**: Start by eliminating any high-interest debt, such as credit card balances, as this type of debt can eat away at your wealth-building efforts.

- **Creating an emergency fund**: Save three to six months' worth of living expenses in a liquid, easily accessible account. This will serve as a financial safety net in case of unexpected expenses or a loss of income.

- **Budgeting and controlling expenses**: Living below your means is critical for building wealth. Track your income and expenses carefully and look for ways to cut unnecessary costs to free up more money for savings and investments.

Proverbs 6:6-8 (NIV) encourages us to learn from the ant's example of preparation and hard work: "*Go to the ant, you sluggard; consider its ways and be wise! It has no commander, no overseer or ruler, yet it stores its provisions in summer and gathers its food at harvest.*" This verse reminds us of the importance of preparing for the future and laying a strong financial foundation.

3. Maximize Your Savings Rate

One of the most important factors in achieving financial independence is saving as much as possible.

The higher your savings rate, the faster you can accumulate the wealth needed to reach financial independence. Many financially independent individuals save 50% or more of their income.

To maximize your savings rate:

- **Cut unnecessary expenses**: Review your spending habits and look for areas where you can reduce costs, such as dining out less frequently, downsizing your home, or cutting subscriptions.

- **Increase your income**: Look for ways to boost your earnings, such as taking on a side hustle, freelancing, or negotiating a raise at your current job.

- **Avoid lifestyle inflation**: As your income increases, resist the temptation to upgrade your lifestyle. Instead, channel the extra income into savings and investments.

4. Invest Wisely for Growth

Achieving financial independence requires growing your wealth over time through smart investments.

Simply saving money in a low-interest savings account will not be enough to reach your goals. Instead, you need to invest in assets that offer higher returns, such as:

- **Stocks and bonds**: Investing in a diversified portfolio of stocks and bonds allows you to grow your wealth through market appreciation and dividends.

- **Real estate**: Rental properties can generate passive income through rent, while the value of the property appreciates over time.

- **Mutual funds or index funds**: These funds provide a way to diversify your investments while keeping costs low, making them ideal for long-term growth.

The key to successful investing is to take a long-term approach and avoid trying to time the market. Stay invested, reinvest your dividends, and take advantage of compound interest to grow your wealth over time.

Proverbs 21:20 (NIV) advises: "*The wise store up choice food and olive oil, but fools gulp theirs down.*" This verse speaks to the wisdom of saving and investing for the future, rather than spending everything you earn in the present.

5. Create Passive Income Streams

One of the defining characteristics of financial independence is having multiple streams of passive income—income that is generated without active involvement. Passive income can come from various sources, such as:

- **Investments**: Stocks, bonds, and real estate that generate income through dividends, interest, or rent.

- **Online businesses**: Creating digital products, such as eBooks, online courses, or software, that can be sold repeatedly with minimal ongoing effort.

- **Royalties**: Earning royalties from intellectual property, such as books, music, or inventions.

Creating passive income streams is essential because it allows you to generate income even after you stop working. By building and growing these income streams, you can eventually cover all your living expenses without relying on traditional employment.

In conclusion, financial independence is about achieving the freedom to live life on your terms, without the need to actively work for income. By understanding the difference between financial freedom and independence; and following the steps to build a strong financial foundation, maximize your savings, invest wisely, and create passive income streams, you can reach financial independence and secure your financial future. Proverbs 24:27 (NIV) offers timely advice: "*Put your outdoor work in order and get your fields ready; after that, build your house.*" This scripture emphasizes the importance of preparation and careful planning—essential steps in the journey to financial independence.

Chapter 11: Retirement Planning and Life Insurance

Planning for retirement and securing the future of your loved ones with life insurance are two critical components of a solid financial strategy. Retirement accounts help you save for the future, while life insurance provides financial security to your family in case of your passing. This chapter will provide an overview of popular retirement accounts, such as RRSPs, TFSAs, and 401(k)s, and highlight the importance of choosing the right life insurance plan to protect your family.

Understanding Retirement Accounts: RRSPs, TFSAs, and 401(k)s

Saving for retirement is one of the most important financial goals you can set. However, choosing the right retirement account is crucial to making sure your savings grow effectively over time. Different countries offer various types of retirement accounts, each with its own tax advantages and benefits. Below, we explore the most common retirement accounts used in Canada and the United States.

1. RRSPs (Registered Retirement Savings Plans) – Canada

The **Registered Retirement Savings Plan (RRSP)** is a tax-advantaged retirement savings account available to Canadian residents. It allows you to contribute a portion of your income into the account, and your contributions are tax-deductible. This means that the amount you contribute reduces your taxable income for the year, allowing you to save on taxes.

Key benefits of RRSPs include:

- **Tax-deferred growth**: Investments within an RRSP grow tax-free until you withdraw them. This allows your savings to compound over time without being eroded by taxes.

- **Taxation on withdrawal**: When you withdraw funds from your RRSP during retirement, the amount is taxed as regular income. However, most retirees are in a lower tax bracket than they were during their working years, so they typically pay less tax on withdrawals.

RRSPs are particularly beneficial for individuals who expect to be in a lower tax bracket during retirement than they are now. By deferring taxes until retirement, you allow your investments to grow tax-free for many years.

2. TFSAs (Tax-Free Savings Accounts) – Canada

The **Tax-Free Savings Account (TFSA)** is another retirement savings vehicle available to Canadians. Unlike RRSPs, contributions to a TFSA are not tax-deductible, but the growth within the account and all withdrawals are completely tax-free.

Key benefits of TFSAs include:

- **Tax-free growth**: Any interest, dividends, or capital gains earned within a TFSA are not subject to taxes, allowing your money to grow faster.

- **No tax on withdrawals**: Unlike RRSPs, withdrawals from a TFSA are not taxed. This makes it a flexible savings account that can be used for both short-term and long-term goals, including retirement.

A TFSA is ideal for individuals who expect to be in the same or higher tax bracket during retirement, as it allows them to withdraw money without facing tax penalties.

Proverbs 21:5 (NIV) provides wisdom about diligent saving: "*The plans of the diligent lead to profit as surely as haste leads to poverty.*" By carefully planning your retirement savings through RRSPs and TFSAs, you can ensure financial stability in the later years of your life.

3. 401(k)s – United States

The 401(k) is one of the most popular retirement savings plans available to U.S. workers. It allows employees to contribute a portion of their pre-tax income into the account, reducing their taxable income for the year. Many employers offer matching contributions, further boosting the amount saved.

Key benefits of 401(k)s include:

- **Tax-deferred growth**: Like RRSPs, the money in a 401(k) grows tax-free until it is withdrawn. This allows your investments to benefit from compounding without tax interference.

- **Employer matching**: Many employers match a percentage of the contributions you make to your 401(k), essentially offering free money to help grow your retirement savings.

However, 401(k) funds are taxed as regular income when withdrawn during retirement. There is also a Roth 401(k) option, which allows you to contribute after-tax dollars, meaning withdrawals during retirement are tax-free.

The Importance of Life Insurance and How to Choose the Right Plan

While retirement planning focuses on ensuring you have enough money to live comfortably in your later years, life insurance ensures that your family is financially protected in case of your passing. Understanding how life insurance works and choosing the right plan is essential to securing your loved ones' financial future.

1. Why Life Insurance is Important

Life insurance is designed to provide financial support to your beneficiaries (usually your family) in the event of your death. If you are the primary breadwinner or have dependents, life insurance can help cover expenses such as:

- **Funeral costs**: Life insurance can cover the expenses related to your funeral and burial.

- **Outstanding debts**: It can help pay off mortgages, car loans, and other debts that your family might struggle with after your passing.

- **Living expenses**: Life insurance ensures that your family can maintain their standard of living by providing income replacement.

- **Future financial goals**: It can also fund long-term goals such as your children's education or your spouse's retirement.

Proverbs 13:22 (NIV) emphasizes the importance of leaving a legacy for your family: *"A good person leaves an inheritance for their children's children.*" Life insurance allows you to fulfill this biblical principle by ensuring that your loved ones are taken care of financially after you are gone.

2. Types of Life Insurance

There are two main types of life insurance to consider: **term life insurance** and **permanent life insurance**.

- **Term Life Insurance**: This type of insurance provides coverage for a specific period, such as 10, 20, or 30 years. It is generally more affordable and is ideal for individuals who want coverage during their working years when their financial obligations are higher (e.g., raising children, paying off a mortgage). If the policyholder dies during the term, the insurance pays out a death benefit to the beneficiaries. However, if the policy expires before the policyholder's death, no benefits are paid.

- **Permanent Life Insurance**: This type of insurance provides lifelong coverage and includes a **cash value** component that grows over time. While the premiums for permanent life insurance are higher than for term life insurance, it can accumulate savings that can be borrowed against or withdrawn during your lifetime. Types of permanent life insurance include **whole life** and **universal life** insurance.

3. How to Choose the Right Life Insurance Plan

Choosing the right life insurance plan depends on several factors, including your financial situation, your family's needs, and your long-term goals. Here are some steps to guide you in making the right choice:

- **Assess your financial responsibilities**: Consider the amount of income your family would need to replace in your absence. This includes outstanding debts, living expenses, and future goals like college tuition.

- **Determine the length of coverage**: If you only need life insurance for a specific period (e.g., until your children are grown or your mortgage is paid off), a term life insurance policy might be the best option. If you want lifelong coverage and the opportunity to build cash value, a permanent policy might be more appropriate.

- **Compare premiums**: Make sure to choose a policy with premiums that fit within your budget. Term life insurance typically offers lower premiums, but permanent policies can provide additional benefits, such as cash value accumulation.

- **Consult a financial advisor**: It's always a good idea to speak with a financial advisor to ensure that you choose the right policy for your specific needs.

Proverbs 27:12 (NIV) offers wisdom on foresight and preparation: *"The prudent see danger and take refuge, but the simple keep going and pay the penalty."* By securing life insurance, you are taking prudent steps to protect your family from financial hardship in the event of the unexpected.

In conclusion, retirement planning and life insurance are two essential components of a sound financial strategy. By taking advantage of retirement accounts like RRSPs, TFSAs, and 401(k)s, and securing the right life insurance plan, you can ensure both a comfortable retirement and the financial security of your loved ones. By planning for the future and making wise decisions now, you are building a legacy that will protect and provide for your family for years to come.

PART 5: CHANGING YOUR FINANCIAL MINDSET

Chapter 12: From Paycheck Mentality to Net Worth Mentality

Many people focus exclusively on their income—the amount of money they bring in from their job each month—believing that earning more is the key to financial success. However, focusing solely on income is not enough to build wealth. To truly achieve financial security and long-term success, it's important to shift your mindset from a paycheck mentality to a net worth mentality. This chapter will explore the importance of making this shift, focusing not just on earning but on building wealth and why changing your financial mindset is crucial for achieving lasting financial success.

Shifting from Focusing on Income to Building Wealth

A **paycheck mentality** is the mindset that views financial success as simply earning a regular income and covering expenses. This is a common approach, especially for individuals who work paycheck to paycheck, focusing primarily on their monthly earnings to meet immediate financial needs. While income is important, relying solely on it can limit long-term financial growth.

A more powerful approach is adopting a **net worth mentality**, which focuses not just on income but on building wealth. **Net worth** is the total value of all your assets (such as savings, investments, and property) minus your liabilities (debts). Shifting your focus from how much money you earn to how much wealth you accumulate will fundamentally change your financial outlook and strategy.

1. The Limits of Focusing Solely on Income

While earning a higher income can improve your financial situation, it does not automatically lead to wealth. Many people with high incomes still struggle financially because they spend as much—or more—than they earn. This phenomenon is often referred to as lifestyle inflation: as income increases, so do expenses, resulting in little to no improvement in net worth.

A paycheck mentality can trap individuals in the cycle of constantly seeking higher-paying jobs or promotions without focusing on how to grow and protect their wealth. When financial emergencies arise, people with a paycheck mentality may find themselves unprepared, having neglected to save or invest their income for the long term.

Proverbs 21:20 (NIV) reminds us of the wisdom in accumulating wealth rather than spending it all: *"The wise store up choice food and olive oil, but fools gulp theirs down."* This scripture underscores the importance of saving and building wealth rather than consuming everything you earn.

2. The Power of a Net Worth Mentality

A net worth mentality, on the other hand, focuses on building and growing your assets over time. Rather than simply earning money and spending it, this mindset encourages you to:

- **Save and invest** a portion of your income regularly.

- **Build assets** like investments, real estate, and savings that appreciate over time.

- **Reduce liabilities** by paying off debt and avoiding unnecessary loans.

When you prioritize building your net worth, you are working toward financial independence. Your goal is not just to earn money today, but to create wealth that will sustain you for the future, grow passively, and be available for unexpected expenses or long-term goals like retirement.

In practical terms, this means making decisions that increase the value of your assets. Instead of purchasing luxury goods or upgrading your lifestyle with every income increase, focus on purchasing assets that will appreciate or generate additional income, such as stocks, bonds, or rental properties. Over time, your assets will grow, and your net worth will increase, regardless of fluctuations in your paycheck.

Why Financial Mindset Matters for Long-Term Success

Your financial mindset—the way you think about and approach money—has a profound impact on your long-term financial success. Adopting a net worth mentality not only helps you grow your wealth, but it also changes the way you handle your finances day to day. Understanding why this mindset shift is crucial for long-term success can help you make better financial decisions that support lasting prosperity.

1. Shaping Your Financial Habits

Your mindset directly influences your financial habits. Those with a paycheck mentality may be more likely to spend impulsively, focus on short-term gains, and neglect long-term financial planning. On the other hand, a net worth mentality encourages you to think about the future and develop habits that contribute to financial growth, such as:

- **Consistently saving** a portion of your income, no matter how small.

- **Investing** in assets that appreciate over time or generate passive income.

- **Tracking your net worth** regularly to monitor your financial progress.

- **Avoiding unnecessary debt** and living within your means.

When you have a net worth mentality, you view every financial decision through the lens of how it affects your long-term wealth. This shift in thinking helps you make smarter choices, whether it's deciding to invest in the stock market instead of making a large purchase or paying off debt instead of accumulating more.

Proverbs 13:11 (NIV) teaches: *"Dishonest money dwindles away, but whoever gathers money little by little makes it grow."* This scripture reinforces the value of slow, steady wealth-building over time, which is central to a net worth mentality.

2. Achieving Financial Independence

A net worth mentality is essential for achieving **financial independence**—the point at which you no longer rely on active income (such as a paycheck) to support your lifestyle. Financial independence is the result of consistently building your net worth over time by growing your assets and reducing your liabilities.

Financial independence gives you the freedom to make life decisions without being constrained by financial concerns. Whether you want to retire early, pursue a passion project, or spend more time with family, a net worth mentality helps you create the financial stability and freedom to live life on your own terms.

3. Planning for Generational Wealth

A paycheck mentality focuses on immediate needs, but a net worth mentality allows you to think beyond your lifetime. Building generational wealth—wealth that can be passed down to future generations—requires long-term planning and a mindset focused on accumulating and preserving assets.

By adopting a net worth mentality, you not only secure your own financial future but also create opportunities for your children and grandchildren. Proverbs 13:22 (NIV) reminds us: *"A good person leaves an inheritance for their children's children."* This verse emphasizes the importance of thinking beyond the present and working to provide for future generations.

Practical Steps to Shift from a Paycheck to a Net Worth Mentality

Making the shift from a paycheck mentality to a net worth mentality requires intentional action. Here are practical steps you can take to start building wealth and changing your financial mindset:

1. Track Your Net Worth

Start by calculating your net worth: the total value of your assets (savings, investments, real estate, etc.) minus your liabilities (debts, loans, mortgages). Tracking your net worth regularly will help you see how your financial decisions are affecting your wealth over time. Use a simple spreadsheet or a financial app to update your net worth on a monthly or quarterly basis.

2. Focus on Asset Growth

Shift your focus from how much money you are earning to how much wealth you are building. Prioritize asset growth by increasing your investments, purchasing real estate, or contributing to retirement accounts. Every decision you make should be evaluated in terms of how it increases your overall net worth.

3. Minimize Debt

Eliminate high-interest debt as quickly as possible and avoid taking on unnecessary loans. Paying off debt increases your net worth by reducing your liabilities. Once you are debt-free, you can focus on growing your assets without the burden of interest payments.

4. Live Below Your Means

Avoid lifestyle inflation by living below your means, even as your income increases. Instead of spending more as you earn more, continue to save and invest the difference. This discipline will accelerate your wealth-building efforts and help you achieve financial independence sooner.

In conclusion, shifting from a paycheck mentality to a net worth mentality is crucial for long-term financial success. By focusing on building wealth rather than just earning income, you can create financial stability, achieve independence, and provide for future generations. Proverbs 24:3-4 (NIV) offers wisdom on building wealth: *"By wisdom a house is built, and through understanding it is established; through knowledge its rooms are filled with rare and beautiful treasures.*" This scripture reminds us that wealth-building requires wisdom, understanding, and intentional action—principles that are central to developing a net worth mentality.

Chapter 13: Developing Financial Discipline

Financial discipline is the cornerstone of long-term success. No matter how much money you earn or how well you invest, without discipline in managing your finances, your efforts can fall short. **Self-discipline** is what keeps you on track with your financial goals, ensuring that you consistently make wise decisions about spending, saving, and investing. In this chapter, we will explore the role of self-discipline in achieving financial success and offer practical ways to build better financial habits that support your goals.

The Role of Self-Discipline in Financial Success

Financial success is not determined solely by how much money you earn, but by how well you manage that money. This is where self-discipline comes into play. Developing financial discipline requires you to make intentional, often difficult, decisions about how you spend and save money. Without it, even high earners can find themselves in financial trouble, while those with modest incomes can build substantial wealth through disciplined financial management.

1. Avoiding Impulse Spending

One of the greatest obstacles to financial success is **impulse spending**—the tendency to make unplanned purchases without considering their long-term impact on your finances. Impulse spending can derail your budget, deplete your savings, and prevent you from achieving your financial goals. Financial discipline allows you to resist the urge to spend money impulsively and instead focus on your long-term goals.

To avoid impulse spending, it's important to practice **delayed gratification**—the ability to wait and carefully consider your purchases before making them. This means asking yourself whether a purchase is necessary and if it aligns with your financial priorities. Over time, this practice becomes a habit, helping you avoid unnecessary expenses and stay on track with your budget.

Proverbs 21:20 (NIV) reminds us of the consequences of uncontrolled spending: *"The wise store up choice food and olive oil, but fools gulp theirs down."* This verse underscores the importance of saving and being prudent with your resources, rather than spending them frivolously.

2. Sticking to a Budget

A budget is one of the most effective tools for maintaining financial discipline. It provides a clear plan for how to allocate your income toward essential expenses, discretionary spending, savings, and debt repayment. However, creating a budget is only the first step—sticking to it requires self-discipline.

By following a budget, you make sure that every dollar is working toward your financial goals, whether that's paying off debt, building an emergency fund, or investing for the future. Financial discipline helps you resist the temptation to overspend in certain areas, such as dining out or shopping, and instead focus on living within your means.

3. Prioritizing Long-Term Goals Over Short-Term Wants

Another key aspect of financial discipline is learning to prioritize **long-term goals** over **short-term wants**. While it can be tempting to spend money on things that bring immediate gratification, such as vacations or new gadgets, these short-term pleasures can prevent you from reaching more important financial goals, like saving for retirement or buying a home.

Discipline involves making sacrifices today for a better financial future tomorrow. It requires focusing on what truly matters—such as financial independence, debt freedom, or wealth accumulation—rather than being distracted by momentary desires.

Practical Ways to Build Better Financial Habits

Developing financial discipline is a gradual process that requires consistency and commitment. The following are practical strategies to help you build better financial habits and stay on track toward achieving your financial goals.

1. Automate Your Savings

One of the easiest ways to ensure that you consistently save money is by automating your savings. Set up automatic transfers from your checking account to your savings or investment accounts each month, so that a portion of your income is saved before you even have the chance to spend it. This strategy helps you prioritize saving and ensures that you are consistently building wealth without having to rely on willpower alone.

By automating your savings, you remove the temptation to spend the money you should be saving. It also allows you to "pay yourself first" by treating your savings as a non-negotiable expense, just like your rent or utilities.

2. Create a Detailed Financial Plan

A detailed **financial plan** acts as a roadmap for your financial journey. It outlines your goals, sets deadlines for achieving them, and breaks down the steps you need to take to reach them. Having a clear financial plan helps you stay disciplined because it reminds you of your long-term objectives and the importance of sticking to your financial habits.

Your financial plan should include:

- **Short-term goals**: These might include paying off a specific debt, building an emergency fund, or saving for a vacation.

- **Medium-term goals**: This could involve saving for a down payment on a home or funding an education.

- **Long-term goals**: This typically includes retirement savings, investments, and estate planning.

Regularly reviewing and updating your financial plan ensures that it reflects your current financial situation and goals. When you have a plan in place, you are less likely to be swayed by short-term distractions and more likely to stay disciplined.

3. Track Your Spending

Tracking your spending is an essential habit for maintaining financial discipline. By keeping a record of where your money goes each month, you can identify patterns of overspending and make adjustments as needed. Whether you use a budgeting app, a spreadsheet, or even pen and paper, tracking your expenses gives you a clear picture of your spending habits and helps you stay accountable to your budget.

When you track your spending, you also become more aware of your discretionary expenses. For example, you might notice that you're spending more on takeout than you realized, or that your entertainment costs are higher than planned. Once you're aware of these patterns, you can take steps to reduce unnecessary spending and allocate more of your income toward savings or debt repayment.

Proverbs 27:23 (NIV) advises: *"Be sure you know the condition of your flocks, give careful attention to your herds."* This scripture emphasizes the importance of paying attention to your resources, which in modern terms means tracking your finances and staying aware of your spending habits.

4. Set Up a Rewards System

One way to stay motivated and maintain financial discipline is by setting up a **rewards system**. Achieving financial goals, especially long-term ones, can sometimes feel overwhelming. By rewarding yourself for hitting certain milestones, you create a sense of accomplishment that helps keep you on track.

For example, if you've successfully paid off a debt or reached a savings goal, treat yourself to something small that you enjoy, such as a dinner out or a weekend getaway. These rewards provide positive reinforcement and make the process of financial discipline more enjoyable.

5. Surround Yourself with Support

Financial discipline can be challenging to maintain if you are surrounded by influences that encourage spending. One effective strategy is to surround yourself with people who support your financial goals and encourage healthy money habits. This might include a spouse or partner, trusted friends, or even online communities that share advice and support for financial success.

Additionally, consider working with a financial advisor or coach who can provide guidance, help you create a financial plan, and hold you accountable to your goals.

Having someone to help you stay disciplined and focused can make all the difference in your financial journey.

In conclusion, self-discipline plays a crucial role in achieving financial success. By avoiding impulse spending, sticking to a budget, and prioritizing long-term goals over short-term wants, you can develop the discipline needed to reach your financial potential. Implementing practical strategies, such as automating your savings, tracking your spending, and setting up a rewards system, can help you build better financial habits that support your goals. Hebrews 12:11 (NIV) offers encouragement for the value of discipline: "*No discipline seems pleasant at the time, but painful. Later on, however, it produces a harvest of righteousness and peace for those who have been trained by it.*" This verse serves as a reminder that while financial discipline may be difficult at first, the rewards of financial peace and success are well worth the effort.

Conclusion: Taking Control of Your Financial Future

Achieving financial success and security requires not only knowledge but also action. Throughout this book, we have explored the key principles of financial literacy, from budgeting and managing debt to building wealth and planning for retirement. Armed with this knowledge, you now have the tools necessary to take control of your financial future. In this concluding chapter, we will summarize the key financial literacy principles covered, offer encouragement to take proactive steps in managing your finances, and reflect on the lasting importance of financial education.

Summary of Key Financial Literacy Principles

As you reflect on the lessons learned in this book, it's important to remember the foundational principles of financial literacy that will guide you on your journey to financial security and independence:

1. Budgeting and Managing Your Money

Creating and sticking to a budget is one of the most effective tools for managing your finances. By tracking your income and expenses, differentiating between needs and wants, and allocating money toward savings, debt repayment, and investments, you can gain control over your financial situation. A well-planned budget ensures that you live within your means while still working toward your long-term financial goals.

2. Saving and Building an Emergency Fund

Building an emergency fund is crucial for financial stability. Life is full of unexpected expenses, from medical bills to car repairs, and having an emergency fund provides a safety net to cover these costs without relying on debt. Make saving a priority by automating contributions to your savings account and gradually building up to three to six months' worth of living expenses.

3. Reducing and Managing Debt

Debt management is a key part of financial success. Whether it's credit card debt, student loans, or mortgages, understanding how to manage and reduce debt is essential. Prioritize paying off high-interest debt first and avoid taking on unnecessary loans. By reducing debt, you free up more of your income for savings and investments, moving closer to financial independence.

4. Investing for Long-Term Wealth

Investing is one of the most powerful ways to build wealth over time. Whether you're investing in stocks, bonds, real estate, or mutual funds, the key is to take a long-term approach and allow your investments to grow through compound interest. Dollar-cost averaging, diversification, and asset allocation are important strategies that help you manage risk while maximizing returns.

5. Planning for Retirement

Planning for retirement is essential to ensuring financial security in your later years. Take advantage of retirement accounts such as RRSPs, TFSAs, and **401(k)s** to save and invest for the future. The earlier you start, the more time your investments have to grow. By being proactive in your retirement planning, you can ensure that you have enough resources to enjoy a comfortable and fulfilling retirement.

6. Protecting Your Loved Ones with Life Insurance

Life insurance is an important component of a sound financial plan, especially for those with dependents. It provides financial security for your loved ones in the event of your passing, ensuring that they can cover expenses such as funeral costs, outstanding debts, and living expenses. Choosing the right life insurance plan based on your family's needs is critical to providing lasting financial protection.

7. Developing Financial Discipline and Changing Your Mindset

Ultimately, financial success depends on self-discipline and adopting the right financial mindset. Shifting from a paycheck mentality to a net worth mentality helps you focus on building wealth rather than simply earning income. By practicing delayed gratification, setting financial goals, and developing good financial habits, you can achieve long-term financial success and independence.

Encouragement to Take Proactive Steps in Managing Finances

Knowledge is powerful, but it is only truly effective when combined with action. The principles you've learned in this book will only help you if you take proactive steps to implement them in your own life. Here are a few key actions to help you get started on your financial journey:

1. Start Small and Be Consistent

Whether you're building an emergency fund, paying down debt, or investing for the future, start with small, manageable steps. Consistency is more important than size—small, regular contributions to your savings or investments will grow over time. Don't be discouraged if progress seems slow at first. As you develop financial discipline, you'll see your efforts start to pay off.

2. Make Financial Goals a Priority

Set clear financial goals for yourself, both short-term and long-term. Whether it's paying off a credit card, saving for a vacation, or investing for retirement, having concrete goals gives you a sense of direction and purpose. Regularly review your progress toward these goals and adjust your plan as needed.

3. Educate Yourself Continuously

Financial literacy is a lifelong journey. As the world of finance evolves, it's important to continue learning about new investment opportunities, tax laws, and financial strategies. Stay informed by reading financial books, attending workshops, and seeking advice from financial professionals. The more you learn, the better equipped you'll be to make informed decisions about your money.

4. Seek Support and Accountability

Managing finances can sometimes feel overwhelming, but you don't have to do it alone. Consider working with a financial advisor who can help you create a personalized financial plan and hold you accountable to your goals. You can also seek support from family, friends, or financial communities that share similar goals and values. Having a support system can make the journey to financial success easier and more rewarding.

Final Thoughts on the Importance of Financial Education

Financial literacy is the foundation of financial security and success. Unfortunately, many people never receive the education they need to manage their finances effectively. This book has provided you with the essential knowledge and tools to take control of your financial future, but the journey doesn't end here.

Continued financial education is critical to navigating the complexities of personal finance. As you grow in your knowledge and experience, you will be better equipped to make wise financial decisions that benefit you and your family. By taking the time to learn, plan, and act, you can achieve financial independence and create a legacy that lasts for generations.

Proverbs 4:7 (NIV) says, "*The beginning of wisdom is this: Get wisdom. Though it cost all you have, get understanding.*" This verse reminds us that seeking knowledge and understanding is invaluable, especially when it comes to managing our finances. The more you understand about money, the better you can control it and use it to achieve your dreams.

In conclusion, the journey to financial success is one of education, discipline, and action. By applying the principles you've learned, setting clear goals, and taking proactive steps, you can take control of your financial future and build the life you've always envisioned. Remember that the choices you make today will determine your financial stability tomorrow, so start now, stay consistent, and watch your efforts transform your financial landscape for the better.

About the Author

Nick Imoru is a dynamic speaker, author, educator, entrepreneur, and consultant based in Canada. He is the President of Achievers Centre, a division of Philips Reliability Consult Inc. Nick's mission is centered on empowering the human spirit through consulting, coaching, connecting and circulating ideas and information. His goal is to inspire, ignite passion, create profit, and make a spiritual impact, ultimately helping individuals bridge the gap between where they are and where they aspire to be.

Nick holds a B.Eng. in Mechanical and Production Engineering and an MSc. in Advanced Technology from the UK. With over 18 years of experience in the Oil and Gas industry, he specializes in Maintenance & Reliability Engineering and is a Certified Maintenance & Reliability Professional (CMRP), reflecting his commitment to excellence in his field.

As the author of over 20 books and numerous articles and research papers, Nick's work spans personal development, spirituality, academia, business, and finance. He is the founder of Achievers Consult, Achievers Centre, and Achievers Publishing, all operating under Philips Reliability Consult Inc.

Nick is happily married to Dr. Margaret and is a proud father of two daughters, Nelly and Myra. His unwavering dedication to personal and professional growth, combined with his entrepreneurial spirit, continues to make a profound impact on individuals and organizations, guiding them towards success and fulfillment.

With a vision to inspire, train, develop, and unlock potential, Nick Imoru is committed to helping individuals and businesses achieve their highest levels of success.

To contact Nick or learn more about Achievers Centre, opportunities, speeches, and seminars, please use the information below:

Email: Nick@achieverscentre.com
Website: www.achieverscentre.com

Books By Same Author

- A Heart for God
- Operating God's Private Lines
- Growing In Life
- Money & Pleasure: Trap of Purpose
- Success Buttons for Life & Academic Excellence
- The Making of Greatness
- Your Best Year Ever
- Nothing Just Happens
- How Did I Become Like This
- Achievers Daily Tonic
- Living in His Fullness: Unveiling the Life, Mission, Death and Triumph of Jesus
- Your Belief System: How Your Thoughts Dictate Your Life
- The Wit & Wisdom of Dr David Oyedepo
- The Tongue: How Your Words Shape Your Destiny
- He Has Said...So We May Boldly Say
- Character: The Blueprint for a Great Future

- Living in His Light: Understanding Your New Identity in Christ
- Personal & Family Budgeting: Mastering Your Money for Financial Freedom
- Your Money, Your Future: A Student's Guide to Financial Success
- Choosing the Right Path: A Career Guide for Teens and Youth
- The 21 Life Rules Every Child Should Live By
- The Power of Your Environment: How Your Surroundings Shape Your Life
- Think It, Do It: How to Turn Thoughts into Meaningful Action
- Adventures in God's Amazing Storybook, Part 1
- Adventures in God's Amazing Storybook, Part 2

To order any of these books, please visit:

Our online shop @ www.achieverscentre.com

or any of the amazon websites:

www.amazon.ca

www.amazon.com

www.amazon.co.uk, etc

www.ingramcontent.com/pod-product-compliance
Lightning Source LLC
Chambersburg PA
CBHW050001040726
47599CB00014B/1160